EMPOWERED TO
IMPACT

Empowered to Power

FRANK M. BILLUE

Copyright © 2014 by Frank M. Billue

Empowered To Impact
Empowered to Power
by Frank M. Billue

Printed in the United States of America

ISBN 9781498410977

All rights reserved solely by the author. The author guarantees all contents are original and do not infringe upon the legal rights of any other person or work. No part of this book may be reproduced in any form without the permission of the author. The views expressed in this book are not necessarily those of the publisher.

Scripture quotations taken from the New King James Version (NKJV). Copyright © 1982 by Thomas Nelson, Inc. Used by permission. All rights reserved.

www.xulonpress.com

DEDICATION

This book is dedicated to my dear Beloved Wife Marilyn Katrina Billue. To my beautiful wonderful daughters Lucretia, Tracey, and Stephanie, seven grandchildren, one great grandson Kingston.

TABLE OF CONTENTS

Introduction		 vii
Chapter One	*Who Am I*	 11
Chapter Two	How and By Whom Have I Been Empowered	 31
Chapter Three	What is My Calling (Divine Purpose & Destiny)?	 49
Chapter Four	Willing and Obedient To Your Calling	. . . 65
Chapter Five	Legacy (Solidified Remembrance)	 76

EMPOWERED TO IMPACT (MAKE A DIFFERENCE) NOW!
INTRODUCTION

It is amazing to know beyond a shadow of doubt that you and I were created to make a lasting difference in our lifetime and impact generations. Although a marvelous life-long assignment permit me to say to you young people that we are very close to losing a complete generation to illicit sexual promiscuity: babies giving birth to babies, illegal drugs, one-parent, women-headed households, pandemic pornography, and almost every vice (sin) imaginable. Let me be the first to apologize to the young people, for it is us adults—fathers and mothers—who also bear and shoulder much of the accountability and lack of responsibility for where many of you are misaligned and unsynchronized today.

Notwithstanding what I have just stated, and it is the honest truth, there still remains hope and a complete reversible possibility for a transformational turnaround from hopelessness to overwhelming and exceeding perpetual success. Young people, as a believer you serve a God who is able to do exceedingly abundantly above anything we could ask or think. Are you asking God to change and renew your culture and generation? If not, you need to. I charge and challenge every youth age twelve to twenty-one to look at and evaluate your position spiritually and dimensionally. Where are you? What have you been saying to yourself and others? Be very careful of what words enter into your ear-gate; in other words, you cannot allow anyone and everyone to speak into you. This includes the variety of music you listen to. Let the words on the following pages become a constant declaration and command for you to speak for yourself. "For death and life are in the power of the tongue, and those who love it will eat its fruit" (Prv 18:21 NKJV). You will live and not die! Let this be your personal mandate and road map to thrive and succeed in excellence in all God has predestined and ordained for you. Certainly the times are truly evil and there is a great urgency to understand and know you do have a Godly identity with Christ Jesus. Now more than ever it is imperative

Introduction

for you to know who you really are, your identity (DNA). Do not allow uncensored movies, advertisements, extreme, booty-shaking hip-hop music to define your present, past, or future direction; you are created (empowered) to significantly impact your entire generation and environment. Youth, who you are is defined by who God says you are; do not allow TV, BET, commercials and hip-hop to define you or even your peers. Your very presence as a Christian should and must make a difference in our present society and generation of young people. Let's get focused and amped to revolutionize and impact the world....**NOW, LET'S DO IT!** Remember: "Ask not what your country can do for you, but what you can do for your country" (John F. Kennedy). Conversely, remember: "Blessed is the nation whose God is the Lord" (Ps 33:12). Readers, we all truly live in a blessed nation, and it certainly is not because of us but because of God Almighty keeping His unchanging hand on this nation, and because of our reverence and belief in Him and Him alone. We must continue to live up to our acknowledgement that "In God We Do Trust," wholly. Because we trust God, I further challenge you to truly lean on Him, to cast all your cares, concerns and issues on Him, for He cares for us, because He is our good shepherd, and we are the sheep of His great pasture.

EMPOWERED TO IMPACT
BLESSED TO BE A BLESSING
CHAPTER ONE
WHO AM I?

I am a child, son, daughter, king, priest of the Most High God. "I am wonderfully and fearfully made, how marvelous are thy works O God" (Ps 139:14 NKJV). I am an original and not a copy. I am a born-again leader and not a follower. I am a thermostat and not a thermometer; I set the temperature wherever I find myself. I set the standards; I do not accept substandard and stinking thinking ideas or worldly actions. I am a trend setter; that is who I am. I motivate, encourage, and set a standard wherever I am, and I know I am the head. I operate in excellence and not mediocrity. I operate in excellence because I serve an excellent, exact and accurate Savior and Lord. I am both King and Priest. I am the righteousness of

Christ. I have been made righteousness and seated in heavenly places; I have been further blessed with all spiritual blessings in heavenly places. I am ready, willing, obedient and able to execute despite the spiritual warfare that tries to distract and misdirect me. The commands of almighty God are released to me, and I am a soldier in the Army of the Lord Jesus Christ. I refuse to accept the present day familiar, for I realize that in order to catch a draft, I must fish on the opposite side (right side); thus my cast is always in the deep and not the shallow, for the shallow is the <u>familiar</u> and the <u>unfamiliar</u> is the deep.

> Then He got into one of the boats, which was Simon's, and asked him to put out a little from the land. And He sat down and taught the multitudes from the boat. When He had stopped speaking, He said to Simon, "Launch out into the deep and let down your nets for a catch." But Simon answered and said to Him, "Master, we have toiled all night and caught nothing; nevertheless at your word I will let down the net." (Lk 5:3-5 NKJV)

My eyes are lifted to the hills from whence comes my help, for my help comes from the Lord, the Most High God.

Understanding that we are empowered and can do all things through Christ, we are positioned and postured to fully and succinctly understand and identify our covenant connection and relationship with Christ and God Almighty. As such, it is imperative that when we understand who we are and why knowing who we are is so important we are now able to take advantage of every opportunity to influence our immediate, extended and corporate world. Because so many of us have not and were not told who we were during our childhood and even more pronounced today, there is rampant confusion, particularly with many of our youth. Thus, many are seeking steadfastly identification through bling-bling, the latest fashions, hip-hop music, tattooing and all forms of attention-getting schemes to draw attention to them because they have not been loved at home by their biological parents and other relatives who have custody. Readers, youth, it is not about you or us; it's about our Creator, Almighty God. I consider myself one of the fortunate baby-boomers who has never had a problem with understanding who I was (my identity), for my parents instilled in me who I was and who I was not and that I would live-up to their standards because in our home, mediocrity was not the order of the day. Rather, I was always advised that I would not be a failure; instead I would be a significant success or find another roof to live under. My parent's wisdom and insight has been very instrumental in helping me be the godly man I am today.

Now, I realize what I just stated is clearly not the way child rearing is taking place today. However, I can say that their method worked, and while things have become somewhat relaxed today, it is my estimation that societal and successful parenting has experienced an unprecedented record of problem youth today, versus during my era. Youth, readers, with all due respect, I must admit that parenting is better today; nevertheless, the relaxed notions, ideas, value systems and socialization of our youth have suffered tremendously because of a lack of discipline from parents and other adults involved in imparting wisdom into our youth. It is my experience and belief that when youth and adults alike understand, exemplifying a character of knowing who they are through first loving themselves, then there is a domino effect of the same character and action created in every environment in which they find themselves. Thus, knowing who you are drives and propels you to reach your highest potential in every sphere of society—spiritually, socially, financially, educationally and morally. Readers, knowing who you are connects and reconnects you to your spiritual roots and illuminates your pathways to purpose and ultimately your destiny and legacy in this life. Our spiritual roots are that before we became human in an earthly body, we were spirits from God our creator; as such, it is even more important to stay connected to our spiritual beginning— God. Remember, there is only one true and living God, and all other gods are useless idols.

WONDERFULLY AND FEARFULLY MADE

Because I am and you are wonderfully and fearfully made, I fully realize that I am full of ability, insight, direction, power, motivation and influence to make a difference in my generation and beyond. I am a success and not a failure. It will matter that I was born, for I will make a difference in my lifetime. My fearfulness and relevance is solely for my savior and Lord Jesus the Christ and those I come in contact with. I did not create myself; I was created by the intentions and thoughts of my Creator, God almighty. For Jeremiah 29:11 (NKJV) states, paraphrased, "I know the thoughts that I have for you, thoughts of success and not failure, a future and hope."

Because we are wonderfully and fearfully made, we have been created to succeed through the wonderful handiwork of God, and we triumph through His handiwork. Because we all are the handiwork of God Almighty, it should be crystal clear to all of us that we have unlimited potential to succeed, prosper and move toward our purpose with no restrictions. As such, we should be extremely careful and mindful that our bodies are the temples of the Holy Spirit, and we are to treat them accordingly in what we say and do, as well as what we intake of food and drink. Our ability to impact our environment is truly dependent on not only our spiritual health, but also on our natural health. Understanding that truly we are made in the image of God Almighty demonstrates unquestionably we are fearfully and wonderfully made for our Lord and Master Jesus the Christ, the Anointed One with the anointing; for the removal and destruction of yokes, bondages and weights that so easily beset us. Understanding our godly and divine make-up also should eliminate any spirit of fear or inability to accomplish any task or mission set before us; for we are overcomers, conquerors and unstoppable.

An Original and Not a Copy

Many of us, particularly our present hip-hop generation, are seeking to be someone else besides who God created us originally to be. Because all of us are godly originals; created in his image and likeness; we have unlimited potential and solutions built into our DNA. We operate without restrictions supernaturally, doing and performing great exploits because we know and understand the unlimited power of our Great God. Notwithstanding how bad some of us want to be someone else, be yourself, King, Queen, Priest, son, daughter of the Most High God. No one else has what God has gifted you personally; you are one of a kind.

As each of us is an original, you and I have solutions to problems and concerns that only we can solve. Let's be problem solvers. Let's be the solution to issues we were called to be. We are called to be the answer to the issues. The disadvantage is in not being who we have been called to be, but rather a copy of a copy of a copy. Be who you are, for you are unique sons and daughters of God Almighty who is waiting for us to "Arise, shine; for your light has come! And the glory of the Lord is risen upon you" (Is 60:1 NKJV).

Our originality in God should drive and propel us to remain who we were created to be. It appears that maintaining our originality has become problematic in our society in that there are daily attempts to try to duplicate what God created and who He created us to be. Allow me to be very clear: Duplication of God's original intent and purpose cannot be accomplished. Cloning is being done today, but remember, our originality cannot be remade. Regardless of the attempts made, we shall remain who we were originally created to be. Interestingly, society has accepted much drastic and far-reaching human duplication, to be copies of copies rather than remaining to be who we were created to be. This confirms my earlier discussion of the craving to be someone else.

Youth, young people and readers, accept who you are and fulfill your deepest potential, because you are an original and not a copy. You were created in the image and likeness of Almighty God. Remember, when you were formed in your mother's womb the divine pattern was destroyed to maintain your originality.

Leadership

Are you an impactful, influential leader? You absolutely should be. Because of our wonderful and fearful creation, we are spiritually birthed (borne) leaders. Leadership is not a title; rather, it is a spirit and passion birthed spiritually through our acceptance of Christ Jesus. Now, since you understand that you are leaders, what is your responsibility and accountability toward leading, imparting and making a difference that cannot be erased?

As a leader you are responsible to discipline and lead to the purpose and calling of God those who have been placed under and in your sphere of influence. This quite often may mean that I am to disciple other believers, as well as new believers to Christ, through my loving leadership example. Leadership is not easy, for it requires extreme personal sacrifices beyond the call of normal duty. When you become a leader, you give up the right to yourself. This is why the Bible records that the harvest truly is plentiful, but the laborers, workers, (soldiers) leaders are few. This means that true dedicated leaders are few and far between. Additionally, when you fully understand leadership, you give up the right for yourself and are committed to serving and elevating others at the expense of yourself, that's a true leader!

Young people, leaders, please join together in union, realizing that leadership is the ability to share and give out information and influence the way business is conducted. I have found and continue to find that the (your) organization is now ready for forward march into the history of the who, what, where and why we were destined for, the final assessment and victory. It is because leaders lead with influence and consistent results and do not fail at any task, mission or assignment. Like Paul told Timothy, a good soldier must endure hardships; leaders must always be first and move first. For we are the example that everyone is looking toward as being the trendsetters, pathfinders and trailblazers into the twisted world and perilous times we all live in.

Leadership is certainly not easy. Somebody has to be a leader; why not become the leader you were called to be and operate in this wicked world that we live in? Notwithstanding the circumstances, issues and concerns, we must continue to lead steadfastly forward into and through the mind field battles of life. For we do not nor may ever know who is watching us move so they can move out with forward acceleration and consistent momentum and focused victory in alignment and synchronization with Almighty God. Aren't you glad you are no longer in spiritual bondage? Because you are free, the <u>bottom line</u> is for us to <u>seek</u> the <u>Kingdom of God</u> and His <u>righteousness</u> in order that others—our peers, colleagues, friends and relatives—will become free also. Remember, leaders, lead with confidence and assurance. The victory has already been won. First John 5:14 says, "And this is confidence that we have in Him; that if we ask anything according to His will He hears us," and because we know that He hears us we have the petitions and supplications that we desired of Him! Victory!

Follower

Before one can become a leader, one must also have hopefully learned how to be a follower. A follower is one who does not require much direction and will be directed with little to no resistance and supervision. It is my unwavering belief and opinion that followers need direction and with that will probably never operate in a spirit of excellence. Moreover, followers are normally status-quo religious, whereas leaders are always trendsetters and trailblazers. Trailblazers and leaders understand they are empowered, supernaturally energized, to impact and make a difference wherever they are; and furthermore, what's around them and their immediate now environment.

Following a leader and or leaders is a natural instinct that we all have demonstrated at some point in time. Furthermore, a follower will gravitate to his or her natural tendencies as long as the "vision" is not necessarily on us. All readers, please remember a follower is a progressive step toward genuine leadership and management of precious human relationships and resources. Moreover, some look at a follower as a mediocre position or a "0" placeholder well; let me correct that mindset and mentality. This is not necessarily so; again, if you as a follower and are looking to grow and advance, then grow where you are <u>currently</u> planted. Readers', being a follower is very important and should not be discounted in any way or become construed to be diminished because we have limited staff or administrative support. Remember, young people, following is very important and we should not shy away from such an attribute, but rather embrace the requirement and do our very best to meet, succeed and fulfill all requirements.

Making a Difference

Can and should I make a difference as one individual? Yes, you can change if it's only one person.

Understanding we all are empowered to impact and make a difference should and must be the life blood and fuel that launches us into motion to make a difference where we are. Young people, particularly: You have been and are being energized and reenergized by the Holy Spirit to upset, destroy and impact (infiltrate) our entire youth culture today. So with this almighty nonrestrictive now power and authority, you must reign, rule and have dominion; what are you going to do? Well, there are options that are within your sphere of influence to impact, infiltrate, motivate, stimulate, advance, burst forth, and of course, make a difference. Young people, as Christians, regardless of the situation today and seemingly how bad it looks, we are facing the potential and possible loss of a complete generation. What I am saying is that it is always more of us (believers) than it is of them, the un-churched, disobedient, those who are refusing to line up, align themselves with biblical principles and spiritual commandments. It is also further worthy to note that even today many of our churches, as of this writing, are not spiritually conscious and sensitized to the relevance of ministry for this new youth Generation-X culture.

So what do you do? We all, including our youngsters, must aggressively seek and diligently pursue God for creative, innovative ways to reach out and allow the Holy Spirit to arrest youth, for we all are empowered to impact and make a difference. We shall make a difference, and although we are different we must remain the same in what we release in our speaking to our youth. Remaining the same in Christ means we embrace our true supernatural identity. For we are a royal priesthood and a chosen generation; we are peculiar people (youth). So be peculiar in the uniqueness of your Godly creation. Interestingly, as we all move forward in 2014 and beyond, it is becoming intriguing to see and experience how fast everything appears to be and is moving fast forward. The world is in acceleration mode; everything has speeded up to break-neck speed. Where are you? As a youth in this ever-changing information age environment, how do you really make a difference to impact and maintain your values, morals and faith in God, believe and not compromise in or with anything and everything you do. It is worthy to note, young people, all things are possible to them who believe. "Jesus said to him, if you can believe all things are possible to him that believes" (Mk 9:23). Trust; lean on God <u>always</u>. So, if you really desire to shake, impact and rock generations, the opportunity is never more apparent and evident than now. With this in mind, you must follow the leading of the Holy Spirit and your conscience. Following the Holy Spirit and your conscience is a guaranteed confidence and assurance that you will be victorious in everything that you set out to do. For the Holy Spirit will lead and guide you into all truth-Light; thus, you cannot fail in any endeavors you undertake. Conversely, young people, if you follow your own thinking and inclinations, soul, and five senses, then you are surely destined to fail, crash and burn; for the only thing that separates the Soul from the Spirit is the Word of God. Youth, readers, there is life in the word of God, and death in everything else that is not the word of God. "It is the Spirit who gives life; the flesh profits nothing. The words I speak to you are spirit and they are life" (Jn 6:63 NKJV). The scripture records, "For the word of God is living and powerful, and sharper than any two-edged sword, piercing even to the division of soul and spirit" (Heb 4:12 NKJV). What we all really need to understand is that we cannot follow our soul and senses; for we have them and must use them; however, they are not accurate, and we should not depend on them. Ultimately, we must depend on the leading of the Holy Spirit for daily guidance and direction. Allow me to give you an example. Many automobiles today are equipped with Geospatial Positioning Systems (GPS), these systems are magnificent for they will guide you to many destinations, streets, etc. What they cannot do, however, is show you or tell you where the "POT-HOLES" are in the street. Conversely, your soul cannot give the finite detail and direction for your life as the Holy Spirit can and will if you allow Him. I trust that you now see the difference, for the GPS System has the capacity to do many and certain things; however, it is and cannot be omnipresent like the Holy Spirit, for the Scripture says, and I believe as I hope you believe also, that He, the Holy Spirit, will lead you into all (truth) direction and insight. He, the Holy Spirit, does not make any mistakes, for He is everyplace at the same time; the GPS System is not a match or even comparable. As such, even you, young people, having been empowered to make a difference, your ability to make a difference is unlimited. Your ability is unlimited because we believe in and serve a sovereign, almighty, all-powerful God who can and will do everything except fail. Almighty God says in His word that we believers are more than conquerors; for there are more of us (believers) than it is of them, the unbelievers. Youth, as you can visually supernaturally see, everything around all of us is crumbling and falling apart at the seams and foundations. Wars, rumors of wars, earthquakes, mass murders, teenagers, youth killing, maiming, robbing, stealing by youth and adults from their biological parents, teen pregnancy, middle-school lesbianism and homosexuality, children and youth afraid to use the bathrooms for fear of another youth threatening them concerning gangs, and becoming homosexuals, lesbians and the like. What do you suppose is wrong and going on? What is the answer to this confusing, endless,; never-ending madness? Well, I can tell you, it is not looking at more BET, booty shaking, and some of the ungodly hip-hop music degrading, demeaning and demoralizing of women and making them sex objects. Youth, the only temporary and permanent answer is to turn to almighty God. Everyone appears to be perplexed, and even some in despair. Youth, what you must clearly understand is that we believers, children and sons of God walk by faith and not sight. If you see by sight you see the problem, but faith *sees and solves the problem.* Youth, each one of you, not just in the United States of America, but yes, all over the world, are pointed solutions and problem solvers; yes, that is who you are. This is particularly important for you to know now more so than ever before, with the ever-emerging problems of our warped and twisted society today. So let us be about the swift business of solving these present, future, and generational and trans-generational problems we are faced with, for you are walking in the supernatural divine intervention of Almighty God. Understandably, when you truly understand, realize and visualize who you really are, then you will rise up, stand up solve every problem and concern you are confronted with. Young people, you are the future doctors, governmental leaders, scientists, geologists, statisticians, genetics, presidents and entrepreneurs. With this vital understanding, making a difference will become the watch-word for you and your peers. Rather than you receiving the pressure of your peers, you will be inflicting pressure on them to bow to almighty God, be saved, delivered and resurrected in the marvelous light of Godly truth. This idea and concept of making a difference is not some catchy cliché; I'm talking about actually witnessing and experiencing the transforming and mind-renewing power of Almighty God. If you really want to get your life in the true right alignment and synchronization with God, then the only way to do that is get your "THINKING RIGHT." This is not an option or suggestion; rather, it is a commandment from God. You see the scripture records, "For as he thinks in his heart, so is he" (Prv 23:7a NKJV), so as a man/woman; thinks in his/her heart (spirit), so is he/she. Youth, what you think you are is what and who you are. I truly believe that you want to think and be the right person according to who God has created you to be, not what you think or what someone else is attempting to identify you to be. Youth, I remind you: Do not allow others, television or movies to define who you are. I realize our lives are constantly bombarded with all kinds of negativity; however, we can and have overcome. Now, I believe that if all of us just stopped for a moment, we would succinctly realize that what we have been doing to change is not working, <u>spiritually</u>, <u>socially</u>, <u>financially</u> <u>and</u> <u>economically,</u> and what we need to implement is a change in our course and direction or we will not survive the destructive course we are facing. Doing something cannot just be pulled from the sky or by osmosis. Youth, we all must continually seek God and the Holy Spirit as to what we must and should do to make a difference and turn this generation completely around and back to our Creator and Maker. Young people, readers, with this understanding we are destined to not only make a difference, but make a <u>deposit</u> and

<u>impartation</u> for future generations to come. Unfortunately, one of the main reasons that we are now experiencing some of the issues and concerns presently is because our parents and forefathers refused to deal with and make dedicated, committed declarations for their children and their children's children, so they will not experience what we are currently experiencing. Young people, it is our/your turn; let's make a difference and impact our generations and marketplace **NOW**! This is the time and our finest hour.

CHAPTER TWO

HOW AND BY WHOM HAVE I BEEN EMPOWERED?

Young people, you are empowered by our almighty ever-present God. You have the individual ability to reign, rule, and have dominion over anything you are confronted with. Readers, young people, you are more than conquerors. You have and must be exercising the ability to say no to drugs, premarital sex, pornography, sexual promiscuity, and all other vice (sin) while others are succumbing to these deadly and destructive issues, societal issues and concerns. You can say, in fact (SAY IT)—NO! I believe and feel comfortable that you will agree with me; one of the biggest pervasive problems you and I face daily is truly understanding who you are; (Identity Image) who am I? What and who was I created for? What is my purpose? How am I to fulfill my purpose? Who can and will assist me?

What am I to do now? All of these are questions where you are being processed from childhood to adulthood. Youth, first and foremost, you must understand that you have been created in the image/likeness of God. Now, I'm sure you are asking; who am I really? Yes, you are a human being, but more importantly, you are vessels and instruments of honor, not dishonor. Thus, you must act responsibly and accordingly. Now let me tell you who you really are not. Young people, you are not bling-bling, name-brand shoes and clothing. Never allow any of what I have described to define who you are or even somebody else defining who they think you are. Please understand that you have been created in the image of Almighty God. That means that you have been created in the likeness and image of God.

Young people, you are overcomers and conquerors; you are inventors, solutions to complex and unanswered problems and situations in our society; as a matter of fact, our Lord and savior has invested His life in us, so God is expecting a reasonable return on His investment of us in a reasonable amount of time. Youth, while you are chronologically young today, if you keep having birthdays you will become old. What I'm really saying is that every day of our lives we must be focused and productive toward fulfilling our God-given talents, life goals, objectives and godly purpose. Hopefully we understand that what we are doing today is preparing us for how we will operate in eternity everlasting.

I am empowered by Almighty God and the Holy Spirit, and because of my empowerment, I will not succumb to or be entangled with any societal concerns or focus on worldly (carnal) mindsets. While I am in the world, I understand that I must deal with and navigate through the minefield of this temporal life. Nevertheless, I will not be bound by man's limitations of operating by only our five senses, taste, touch, smell, sight and hearing. While these are necessary and needed and were given by Almighty God, I am a person of godly faith and will not walk nor allow my character to be driven by what I see with my physical eyesight. Because of my empowerment, I believe I can do all things through Christ Jesus who perpetually strengthens me in my going and coming daily. As I am strengthened, I am able to encourage and pass along the strength of our empowerment to the less fortunate, as well as these who may have experienced some temporary setbacks or stumbling blocks, through my understanding how and why I have been empowered. It is ever the more important to me to pray and fast so that I will not be overcome by any circumstances or situations.

Finally, my empowerment has taught me that it is not necessarily for me; rather, it is for those who I come in contact with. My purpose is to empower, influence, impact those I come in contact with.

IMAGE

Because I now understand who I am, I now see and visualize my true purpose and why I was created in the image and likeness of Almighty God. Understanding my image and who I am will give me a different perspective of what God expects others to really see in me and how they see and are in contact with me. Others—peers, friends, neighbors and family—should see and experience God-like character and behavior in me. This character and behavior should manifest itself in the form of humility, <u>unconditional love</u>, <u>long-suffering</u>, <u>forgiveness</u> and be desensitized to any offence.

I believe and hope you agree one of the big solutions in the body of Christ is knowing that we have been empowered to impact. There are too many godly soldiers wounded on the battlefield who will not and cannot get up because of offence. This to a very large degree has almost immobilized fast forward movement and greater works of the church. Readers, youth, this syndrome and phenomenon must cease and desist if we, the church, are to move forward and impact our dying world. Readers, we are the answers to this ever-present dilemma. Let's be about the business of eliminating this temporary challenge before it becomes a permanent fixture in our mind.

WHO DO I SEE MYSELF AS?

As believers of the Most High God, young people, you must have a godly revelation and vision; you must know, view, and envision yourself as a success and not a failure. Young people, you are conquerors and overcomers in everything you engage in. Because you are on the team that won, you have already overcome; you are not overcoming; thus your victory is in your continual obedience, knowing that you are a victor and not a victim of any internal or external worldly and social or societal circumstances. You are confronted, for instance, if you are in high school, you are a graduate and not a drop-out; if you are in trade school, you are a success, and you will graduate, because you are a victor, you will not experiment with drugs, premarital sex, pornography or any other vice (sin) that will adversely affect your God-given image; you are a winner, not a loser. You have been created in the image (likeness) of almighty God; and you will not change who you are because you are an original and not a copy, so remain who you are and who you were created to be. I trust that we all see ourselves as the visible manifestation of the invisible God. If we see ourselves as little gods and we are; Psalm 82 says God stands in the congregation of the mighty; He judges among the gods. How long will you judge unjustly and show partiality to the wicked? Selah. Defend the poor and fatherless; do justice to the afflicted and needy. Deliver the poor and needy; free *them* from the hand of the wicked. They do not know, nor do they understand; they walk about in darkness; all the foundations of the earth are unstable. I said, "You *are* gods, and all of you *are* children of the Most High. But you shall die like men, and fall like one of the princes." Arise, O God, judge the earth; for you shall inherit all nations. Then we have a clear and full revelation of who the majestic and awesome God is, today, tomorrow and forevermore. Thus, this will keep me in the thought process and mindset that I am and was created to be an original of Almighty God. See yourselves as God sees you, a victorious overcomer!

ABILITIES

Because you have been created in the image likeness of almighty God, you have unlimited, unrestricted potential and creative power and ability. There are no tasks, desires, situations, circumstances or obstacles that can prevent you from succeeding and overcoming in this present life. God has pre-destined and destined you to be a success; the only person who can stop you and your destiny is you. Young people, activate and employ the almighty power of God in every area of your life <u>now</u>. As trivial as it may seem to some of you, God is concerned with every finite detail of our life; furthermore, he is intimately concerned that you succeed in every area of your life, no matter how small or large the task, situation or circumstance you are engaged in. For it can be a test in high school, middle school, driver education test, a particular subject test; whatever it may or may not be, you have the inherent God given power and ability to overcome with triumphant victory. So get with the program of being a pace- and trend-setter in everything that you put your hands to, for you are a winner and overcomer. Everything that you put your hands to must prosper for the glory (fullness) of God in and upon you. Also, because you are victors, you should and must be able to empower and significantly impact others because they are not as confident and courageous as you. Because you are a king's son or daughter, you have been born with unlimited potential and problem-solving attributes and you can do nothing but prosper and advance spiritually, morally and economically in this life and generation through empowering and impacting others. Because of the confusion and instability of our present-day world, the whole earth is groaning with birth pangs for the true sons of God to rise up. Readers/young people, we need to rise up, shine and be what God has created us to be. Now is the time; let's move forward.

Because you understand you have unrestricted potential, God has no limitations on you. The only limitations are created by you attempting to reason your way through difficult situations and circumstances; rather than believing and accepting all things by faith and not by sight. Through me abstaining from reasoning and speaking what is not as though it was (Rom 4:17);(as it is written, "I have made you a father of many nations") in the presence of Him whom he believed—Through God who gives life to the dead and calls those things which do not exist as though they did, I am now able to speak, enforce, and command supernatural outcomes for me, my peers, family and all these I have come in contact with. Remember, my abilities are not my own; they are for others and must be used for the same.

TALENTS/CHARACTER

Young people, everything that you need and desire you already have from birth, for the Kingdom of God is in you. The only issue is that you (young people) get the revelation (vision) that you are to release and activate your God-given talents wherever you are. Also, please understand your talents will surely get and give you boldness and access to unusual opportunities in life, v:s-v:s sports, scholarships, travel, all kinds of monetary and non-monetary awards and declarations; however, the only thing that will keep, maintain and sustain you is your character. Remember, your character is who you are when no one is watching. Now, I know that you are asking, what is my character? Young people your character is your daily walk (Christian); your character is what you do when no one is looking. What happens when you supposedly are out of sight and behind closed doors? Remember, if you abuse and misuse the God-given talents and decide to walk in disobedience, these talents will be taken away from you and given to someone else who will use them for the glory of God.

It is very important that whatever you do with the talents and gifts you have been given to use them as unto the Lord and not to men; for only what you do for God will last. Moreover, while your talents will open doors for you, only your character will keep you where your talents cannot. I know you are asking, what are you saying and what do you mean? Glad you asked, and let me add, that's a very good question. Remember, your character is who you are and what you do when nobody is looking, whereas your gifts and talent are what God has given to you that can be seen and manifested in the natural by the supernatural spirit of the Living God. This is why it is so important for all of us to watch, pray and seek help, counsel, guidance and direction of the Almighty to help us when we are by ourselves that we will not succumb to or become overwhelmed by worldly and temporal temptations that will tarnish and bring our character into question. Remember always that a great name is better than riches and wealth. For our name always precedes us; it goes before and arrives even before we do. That's why you never do anything in the dark that you do not want brought to the light of truth. For once your name and character had a bad, dark past; it is very difficult to regain the greatness or notoriety that you once had. While

God Almighty forgives us, man in his inability harbors mistakes that we make and attempt to hold us in their bondage for years in many instances. So I say to you, keep it clean—always. That way you will not spend an inordinate amount of time to correct/gloss over some minor character flaw that could be detrimental to your entire life, growth and development. It is amazing how man has an uncanny way of remembering all of the bad about us and so easily forgets the good that we in many cases spend our lifetime's journey creating. Yet in one simple instant/mistake, it can be ruined because we mistake our talent for character.

GIFTING

You are supernaturally gifted and empowered beyond your natural imagination and ability. Well, I am sure you are asking, and I'm glad you are, where these gifts are and what to do with them. Youth, first and foremost understand that the gifts you have, have been freely given and released by God spiritually and supernaturally. These gifts are both supernatural and natural.

The supernatural gifts include preacher, teacher, apostle, prophet, and evangelist. Now, you may be thinking, as well as saying, I do not want these gifts; I do not want to be one of these individuals; and furthermore, I am not willing to accept the <u>responsibility</u> and <u>accountability</u> that comes with them. Also, I'm sure you are also asking or thinking, I want to be gifted with and operate with what the world offers and what this present age is doing. Young people, you have the same and similar gifting as you see in normal people; however, discovering and operating in your God-given gifting is what you do not want to miss, for this is your destiny, legacy and purpose for being in this time and age. So, again, I'm sure you are asking and feeling somewhat concerned. What is my gifting? How am I to discover, uncover, my gifting? The only way to discover and operate in your gifting is to seek the (Holy Spirit) the supernatural to what the gifts are and when they are to be implemented in your life. Once you discover and uncover what the gifts are, you must trust almighty God for these gifts and the manifestation and evidence of them in your daily life from youth to adulthood. Youth, the gifts are not for you; they are for those we are anointed (empowered) to impact in this life. Youth, use your gifts now and see the evidence of the almighty God manifest the miraculous and supernatural in your life and the lives of those you are to touch and impact.

Because you are gifted, there are individuals in your garden and sphere of influence only you can touch. This is true because through your God-given gifting you are the only one who has been given the "keys of authority" to unlock their locked up situations and circumstances. Moreover, because you are gifted and have been delivered in a particular area, you possess "keys" to unlock their similar situations, issues and concerns. As you probably already know, gifts are not earned or deserved. They are freely given, released by Almighty God to be given to others for their deliverance, healing, wholeness and restoration.

Too many of our misunderstandings of our gifts are beyond our imagination. We all have been embedded with gifts. These gifts are to be used to advance and further the Kingdom of God in the earthly realm—our houses, businesses and in the marketplace. Now, since you realize you have gifts, use them wisely, with the utmost reverence and humility, for they are precious in the sight of almighty God.

MEDIOCRE OR EXCELLENCE

Youth, I have a question for you; are you mediocre or excellent? Is your life victorious or marred by daily defeat? Young people, when you fully realize you are <u>kings</u>, <u>priests</u>, and <u>more</u>

than conquerors, you must always operate in the (spirit) of the supernatural spirit of excellence and never mediocrity. Mediocre means just getting by and doing minimum. For example, working a job (just over broke) rather than operating in the excellence of God and His Almighty Kingdom, which is indicative of having more than enough, God gives us abundant grace. "And God is able to make all grace abound toward you, that you always having all sufficiency in all things; may have an abundance; for every good work" (2 Cor 9:8 NKJV). The kingdom represents excellence, not mediocrity. In the kingdom, there is not only the excellence of God, but there is also His exceeding surpassing greatness, abundance and goodness; God is our exceeding great reward. Furthermore, as you operate in the excellence of God, you will <u>experience</u> and <u>understand</u> that there truly are no limits and no boundaries with the supernatural of God. We will not be singing this song; we will encounter unlimited blessings. This will not just be something you talk about only; rather, it will manifest through evidence and demonstration in your daily lives. The sky is the limit, and seemingly impossible tasks or challenges through God are possible, not impossible. Many of you have been taught—and some of you are still being taught—that <u>going to school, getting an education</u> and getting a good job equates to making a lot of money. Well, this statement communicated by our wonderful parents indeed reveals their sincerity, but this is far from the truth. The statement is not one of reality for most of us and has certainly not happened; a good education has not necessarily realized richness or wealth. Please understand that an education is needed in our society. However, it will not necessarily bring wealth and riches. As a matter of fact, there are college dropouts who are making more money and are far richer than some college graduates. Please also understand the difference between wealth and riches. Riches are material holdings, whereas wealth is wisdom and intangibles.

Let me challenge your thinking with this; most of us even today find ourselves with jobs that are mediocre rather than operating in the excellence of God. As a beginner in school or a career, you may start out mediocre, but please do not <u>homestead</u>, <u>tabernacle</u>, and major in just getting by; rather, understand that God and God alone is the source, <u>sustainer</u> and <u>maintainer</u> of your life, and you will operate in nothing less than his excellence in all things. It's your choice and you can do it. You will make an impact and lasting mark that cannot be erased. For you and "I can do all things through Christ which strengthen us" (Phil 4:13 NKJV). I will lift (raise) my eyes (vision) to the hills (high places) from whence cometh my help, for my helps comes from the Lord, the most high God.

> He who dwells in the secret place of the Most High shall abide under the shadow of the Almighty. I will say of the Lord, He is my refuge and my fortress; My God, in Him I will trust. Surely, He shall deliver you from the snare of the fowler and from the perilous pestilence. He shall cover you with His feathers, and under His wings you shall take refuge; his truth shall be your shield and buckler. You shall not be afraid of the terror by night, or of the arrow that flies by day, nor of the pestilence that walks in darkness. Nor of the destruction that lays waste at noonday. A thousand may fall at your side, and ten thousand at your right hand; but it shall not come near you. Only with your eyes you look, and see the reward of the wicked. Because you have made the Lord, who is my refuge, even the most high, your dwelling place, no evil shall befall you, nor shall any plague come near your dwelling; for He shall give His angels charge over you, to keep you in all your ways. In their hands they shall bear you up, lest you dash your foot against a

stone. You shall tread upon the lion and the cobra, the young lion and the serpent you shall trample underfoot. Because he has set his love upon me, therefore I will deliver him; I will set him on high, because he has known my name. He shall call upon me, and I will answer him, I will be with him in trouble; I will deliver him and honor him. With long life I will satisfy him, and show him my salvation. (Ps 91 NKJV)

Because I now understand that I was born to make a difference and be different, just getting by, doing the minimum (mediocre) and not operating in a spirit of excellence is now past tense. Young people, you are more than conquerors; you are lenders, not borrowers; you are leaders, not followers. You are trailblazers and trendsetters, so with this understanding, <u>operate</u>, <u>evaluate</u>, <u>access</u> and size up every situation to be one that you will operate in a spirit of excellence; unsurpassed and second to none. Everything you have been ordained to accomplish, you will rise to the occasion in surpassing victory and excellence because you are destined to impact your generation. Youth, if you are prepared, OPPORTUNITY WILL EXPERTLY MEET preparation both now and in the future. All of us have wasted too much time and too many years. We cannot waste any more years; we all must redeem the times, for the days are extremely evil and unpredictable. We all have been at this mountain too long; it is time to move. If you look closely at our world today, men have become lovers of themselves, more so than God. Tomorrow is certainly not promised to any of us; we must get it right today. Thus, we must all take full advantage of now, for now is always present tense. Youth, do what you can, now, today, not tomorrow, for it is not promised or granted to us. Some of you may be saying, well, I am still young and vibrant; I have plenty of time. Please do not use this scenario. You and all of us only have now; operate in the supernatural now excellence of Almighty God. Allow <u>small, stinking thinking</u> to be a thing of the past;, anything other than operating in excellence is not acceptable, particularly since you are a King's son or daughter. Remember, because you are more than conquerors, operating in excellence is the only mode of your operation and being. Now let's move and execute with the confidence and courage of Almighty God!

CHAPTER THREE
WHAT IS MY CALLING (DIVINE PURPOSE AND DESTINY)?

As Christian believers, we must understand that the most important thing in our lives is to discoverer and fulfill my God-given purpose and destiny and legacy. I must understand and be a living example for those in my garden, sphere of influence; that I did not and could not have come from any big bang theory; rather, I was created by almighty God with a true purpose, destiny and a successful future end. I was and continue to be a thought of God. "I will praise You; for I am fearfully and wonderfully made, Marvelous are your works and that my soul knows very well" (Ps 139:14). The only outstanding issue is for me to <u>discover</u> and <u>uncover</u> what that <u>purpose</u> and <u>destiny</u> is, for it is not easy to discover, but it is possible, and you and others who are not aware of your purpose and destiny, you must immediately seek godly knowledge and godly wisdom from the holy spirit as to what that purpose and destiny are. That is why it is so important to get and maintain a revelation of Almighty God. A revelation of God is a vision of God, an expression of God's character and attributes. God's written word is His revelation.

Youth, your <u>destiny</u> and <u>purpose</u> are so vitally important, for when you find them you have opened the hidden treasures that God predestined for you before you were formed in your mother's womb. With the full understanding of your purpose and destiny, impossibilities become possibilities, immediately and overnight. Mediocre situations and circumstances become excellent visible/light/truth supernaturally. I know some of you are thinking this is not possible; youth, yes, it is possible. Remember, all things are possible to them that believe. "Jesus said to them, if you can believe all things are possible" (Mk 9:23 NJKV). For to believe is to trust, surrender, yield, be confident and assured of what God stated and promised beyond doubt you will witness: the supernatural manifestation and demonstration of the same. Because you have discovered your purpose and destiny, you are now ready, willing and able to be and assist others in doing likewise.

Remember, your purpose is who and what you were created for. Because you have discovered your purpose, you are now ready to operate in your destiny and God will empower you for the same. "And God is able to make all grace abound toward you, that you always having all sufficiency in all things; may have an abundance; for every good work" (2 Cor 9:8).

BEING A CHANGE AGENT

Young people, readers and believers, particularly, we are God's only authorized, legal, authentic agents in the earthly realm for the making of disciples through the spreading of the Gospel. Young people, "if any man be in Christ, he is a new creation" (2 Cor 5:17 NKJV). You are a new creation; and because you now understand your purpose, destiny and legacy, you have become an agent authorized by God to assist others in discovering their purpose and destiny. I know you are again asking, what am I to do to encourage my believing and unbelieving friends, associates, schoolmates and colleagues? Well, because you are operating in the supernatural spirit of excellence, there is an automatic wonder toward what is causing you to prosper (burst/break forth) and advance, and it seems impossible for them. When this occurs, this is now your opportune time to take full advantage of the situation; to witness duplicate your faith in Almighty God, and explain how you <u>discovered</u> and <u>uncovered</u> your purpose and destiny and how it is working and manifesting for you; and that it will concurrently work for others that you come in contact with. Young people, it is just that simple; please do not make it complex. Now, be an authorized change agent, operate in your gifting and exploit (take control) of every imaginable opportunity to facilitate and manifest amazing change (Dn 11:32) (paraphrased) those of us who know our God shall be strong and do great exploits (take over). Doing exploits is not necessarily something we talk about; rather, it is our knowing that our strength, wisdom, insight, direction and confidence must be and remain in Almighty God. Let's do encounter and experience the impossible.

IMPACTING OUR GENERATION

Amazingly, because you now fully understand your purpose and destiny; you are now willing and obedient to impact your generation and make a lasting difference. For you are determined not be a success (according to the world) rather, you/I will be significant; for it will matter when I die, that we were ever born and lived. Moreover, youth you are daily faced with almost blinding insurmountable bombardment of <u>negative media</u>, <u>twenty-four-seven cable-television booty shaking</u>, and <u>rampant murdering</u>, <u>rapes, prostitution</u>, <u>drug dealing</u>, and all kinds of vices (sins) that many of us, including myself, did not have to deal with during our early childhood and adulthood. Nevertheless, even with these inherent and unimaginable problems and difficulties in our present-day society it is still confidently possible to strategically impact this hip-hop generation and make a difference unfathomable. Well, how so? Youth, there has to be that <u>understanding</u>, <u>obedience</u>, <u>determination</u> and <u>steadfastness</u> that I will not succumb to any peer pressure; rather, I will inflict the Almighty Power of God by being a destined leader and not as failing followers of this present age and generation. Now, I know many of you are saying, if I do that, then I am going to be called a square peg in a round hole or some nerd from outer space. Youth, your willingness and tenacity and unwavering determination to impact this generation is unprecedented, necessary and needed. There is an emerging urgency to immediately make a difference, we are about to lose a generation if we do not act now. You know the story; many of us are destroying each other with illicit and illegal drugs and other undisciplined, sinful, devalued habits.

Young people, it is vitally important that you do a self-evaluation assessment of where you are, what you have been listening to, and what you have been looking at and fully evaluate your present position and reposition yourself immediately. Remember your eyes and others are the windows to your soul. Your hearing and intake of some lyrics and music that belong only in the trash cannot be allowed to infiltrate and penetrate your godly temples. Youth, you must turn around and assist others to detour and about face their lives also; if not, we will lose you, and we will not allow this to happen. Stand still (remain in God) and see the salvation (deliverance) of Almighty God. Remember, you can and will impact this generation, for you are empowered (blessed) to be a blessing (empowered) to and for your brothers, sisters and unsaved loved ones. Since most of us are either working or have some interaction, relationship, with the marketplace, this is probably one of the best places to be an example and make a difference. The harvest truly is plenty, but the laborers are few. Also, our colleges, universities, trade schools and institutions for higher learning are fertile ground to be witnesses and make a difference in our seemingly dying nation and world.

Equally important for all of us is to understand and take a vital interest in growing and thriving where we are. Many of us are very discontent and disappointed in the schools we attend, our places of work and even the families we have been born into. Allow me to encourage you that wherever you are you have an opportunity to make a difference, influence and impact individuals, groups and systems for the Kingdom of Almighty God. Let us not procrastinate or hesitate; rather, let us be about the business of actively participating and integrating into their world the Gospel of the Kingdom. I believe that while some of the times we are currently in are the worst of times, some are actually the best of times in that people are seeking, looking for answers to moral issues that cannot and will not be solved by man's intelligence or diverse theory applications. We have reached a plateau and peak in the United States of America, as well as the world. What we have witnessed with our very eyes are <u>unprecedented storms, tsunamis, hurricanes</u> of <u>magnitude proportions</u>, almost <u>financial collapse</u>, moral and spiritual decay never seen before. These issues and concerns will not be solved and settled politically or along any political party lines (for example, Democratic, Republican, Green or Tea Party affiliation). The solution must be and can only come from our Almighty God. Man (natural) has tried and failed. Man's hearts spiritually need to be turned toward God Almighty for the answers and divine direction for the problem solutions to be revealed for solution. So let's seek God and impact our homes, schools, jobs, marketplace and ultimately our world with godly wisdom.

PURPOSE (REASON FOR EXISTENCE)

Young people, hopefully your purpose is not rocket science. It is very simple; it is what you have been called to do during your lifetime, within a reasonable period of time; God expects and demands reasonable progress from all of us. Because you now understand your purpose, you must have an insatiable passion (hunger) and thirst to make a difference. Fulfilling your purpose is not something you do periodically; rather it is a lifestyle. It is not a Sunday event; rather, you do it every day you are alive. No one else can fulfill what you or I are to do other than ourselves. God created our purpose only for us; no one else can do it. There are other youth and adults that only you must, can and should impact and touch. Because you fully understand your purpose, you must work daily and tirelessly to reach your ultimate purpose, which is your destiny and legacy.

DESTINY (MISSION ACCOMPLISHED) COMPLETE

Since you have discovered your ultimate purpose and reason for existence, why you are on planet earth, you can now pursue it with all that you have to impact your generation. For your final purpose, destiny is not a sprint through life, rather it is a marathon (journey) that begins with birth and ends with physical death; yet as a believer, eternal and everlasting life is promised. The most important thing to remember, youth, as a believer is that your physical death is not the end, but rather the beginning of the new and glorified eternal life; that is why it is so important to find your destiny and forge fast forward toward it. Youth, your destiny will propel you into victory after victory after victory.

Always remember destiny is a life long journey of some mountaintop experiences, disappointments, trials, tribulations, mishaps, accidents, but ultimately as a believer of the Lord Jesus Christ, you have the overall victory in life or death, you are overcomers and not losers. Remember, life's journey is just as important as the destination. Because the journey is ongoing, there will be destined and pre-ordained stops and detours along the way. Readers, do not allow the temporary detours and stops to cause you to quit. These detours are to test our faith and endurance to preserve us to the end. Finish the race; you are destined to finish strong.

TEMPORAL VS ETERNAL IMPACT

Because you understand your destiny, a temporal or temporary impact is not sufficient. As people of <u>faith</u>, <u>purpose</u>, and <u>destiny</u>, you must make an eternal impact in your generation now. Well, I'm sure you are asking how to do it. Remembering that your daily life and walk are a living example to and for others to follow allows you to make an indelible and eternal impact on your generation. Now, if you do not understand and change like a chameleon, then you will only make a temporal impact. I think you understand what I am conveying. If you remain <u>constant</u>, <u>focused</u>, <u>persistent</u> and <u>consistent</u>, you will be viewed by your peers as consistent and immoveable, thus effecting an eternal impact on your colleagues. Readers, consistently and persistently realize the victory. Stand still, youth, and see (visualize) perceive the miraculous work of God's almighty power through your steadfastness and consistent actions and behavior. Because you now understand that a temporal impact is temporary, you must make and leave an eternal and lasting impact on your generation and sphere of influence. Understanding that only what you do for Christ will last, you should be elevated in your thinking and belief without any doubt that Christ has made a permanent impact and imprint on you and others. With this understanding, everything that you engage and venture to do must be now (today); it will make such an imprint that even when you die physically, your spirit, supernatural presence, will still remain because of the godly impact of your past presence.

Because this present life is temporal, you must realize that you do not have forever to make a mark on your generation; you must redeem the time, take advantage of every opportunity, for the days are evil. Youth, show up to your assigned position and calling in life and stand. Now, I am sure you are asking, how can and should I make an impact? Moreover, who, what and where am I to impact? Very good question, I am glad you asked. Young people, readers, brothers and sisters, ladies and gentlemen: What you are to impact is to start from where you are now. Whatever assignment you are on, whatever school you are attending, wherever you are in life, start from where you are. Diligently seek God about the specifics—specifically the who, where, how, and when. Remember, wherever you are, your assignment is strategic for you to make a difference and impact the environment so much that even after you leave, your absence of being physically there does not prevent your spiritual presence to still make a continuous impact. Remember, your very physical and spiritual presence makes a difference in others' lives.

Young people of the most-high God, you can and will make a difference. Find out where you are *spiritually*. I am not talking about a physical location, rather a *spiritual position* and dimension and begin slowly but progressively moving forward to change the culture, climate, temperature, and mindset (thinking) of the environment around you and your counterparts and associates. Young people, one thing you must always understand and remember: You are a leader and not a follower. Because you are a leader, you must always set and be the example; you must always exceed all expected expectations. Thus, as you excel, others will and must ask, how are you able to excel while they are always struggling in mediocrity and failure? This may be your only chance to plainly demonstrate and tell them about the Almighty God that you serve,

<u>worship,</u> and <u>praise</u>, who meets your every need, and answers every prayer request. Remember, the world (present-age) society is seeking answers to everything and all things. The whole earth is groaning with birth pains for the saints, sons of the Most High God, to come forth. Young people, it is time for us to come forth. The unfortunate part is that they are looking and seeking for the answers in the wrong places and of the wrong people. Child of God, again this will be and may be your only opportunity to point them to Christ. So do not give out or give up. Maximize every moment. Stay focused on your assignment, goals and objectives, and through your diligence and perseverance many will be saved, disciplined and become soldiers in the army of the Lord.

Now, I am sure you are asking, where do I go from here? Well, you continually duplicate the process and yourself to know and ensure that everyone in your area/sphere of influence is changed and will serve and operate as change agents. Think about it, Soldier: if you or an associate does not make a difference, then things will remain "<u>jacked up,</u>" <u>out of control</u> and "<u>status quo.</u>" The gangbangers, senseless killings, teen rape <u>pregnancy</u>, <u>prostitution</u>, <u>tattooing</u>, <u>body piercing</u>, <u>swelling jails</u> and penal institution population with young black males will continue at an alarming rate. Teens, youth, young adults: Your immediate focus, strategic movement, and now, actions are <u>PARAMOUNT</u> to sweep this <u>nation</u> and the <u>entire globe</u> is so vitally important. Do not be a couch potato, sit and do nothing; rather, make a right now strategic move to help change a generation. Now, please do not take this lightly; your very life, and the life of many other younger adults are at stake, and they are depending on you. We, the world society, cannot afford to experience any more Virginia Techs, Columbines, Aurora, Colorados, or any other senseless and outrageous acts of unprovoked violence and hatred to happen. Please be the change agents that you were called to be even before you were conceived in your mother's womb. Youth, every problem, issue and concern, is and should be all of our concerns. Why? Because we all are affected by what happens in our world. Just think for a moment how 9/11 changed and is continuing to change all of our lives. Things will never be the same again. Young people, allow me to tell you that the building of more <u>jails</u>, <u>prisons</u> and <u>penal institutions</u>, placing metal detectors and other life-altering devices and instruments in our schools and other public facilities are not solving and will not solve the issues we are facing today. The answer is tied up in one thing – God Almighty. <u>People</u>, <u>youth</u>, <u>adults</u> from all walks of life are looking, seeking to find answers and their purpose and to be loved unconditionally. This may appear to be a very simplistic view—and it is—but it is truly the answer. To add to what I believe the answer is, people are seeking their identity. <u>Who am I? Why am I here? What am I here for? What is my purpose?</u> Many, including some of you, have not been told who you are. What am I supposed to be doing and why am I not fulfilled? Believe me, young people: people all over the world are looking for <u>temporal</u> and <u>permanent fulfillment</u>. Without this spiritual supernatural fulfillment, people are <u>empty</u>, <u>confused</u>, <u>distracted</u>, <u>rebellious</u>, <u>angry</u>, <u>depressed</u>, <u>oppressed</u>, and waiting to explode on anyone or thing that gets in their way. This <u>fulfillment</u> can come fortunately through only one Source; that source is God Almighty, our Creator. Single-handedly, the lack of fulfillment is really the largest and most profound problem that we have in our society today. Youth, there is no escape; you must have and receive God before you will have any peace or a fulfilled life. Life begins and ends with our Creator; He finished everything, and then started it with us. Youth, readers, emptiness can and will cause anyone to go over the edge and also take others with them. If we just look at what is happening and what has happened in our society, it will become very evident that extreme issues created by individuals is the direct result of their unfulfilled and spiritually empty and bankrupt lives. Many today are public successes, but they are private failures.

For many of us, young people, you are living for now only, with no <u>thought</u> or <u>imagination</u> that there is or will be an eternity. Well, allow me to refresh your memory a bit. There is an <u>eternity</u>, actually; the <u>eternal</u> is where we all originally came from and certainly all of us will return. <u>Interestingly</u>, in almost all cultures, when the dead is buried, there are references to committing the body back to the Earth; "ashes to ashes," "dust to dust." How you receive and operate in this temporal (Now) time realm, remember you really are planning and preparing as to how you will live out eternity. Our lives and how we live today determines how we will reign and rule in eternity. Young people, this is truly serious business. It is so very important that you find yourself and start walking toward your <u>destiny</u>, <u>purpose</u> and <u>new life</u>, facilitating an <u>individual</u>, <u>collective</u> and <u>lasting impact</u> on your generation and beyond.

CHAPTER FOUR
WILLING AND OBEDIENT TO YOUR CALLING

Because of your persistency and consistency to impact your generation; as well as your obedience and willingness; please realize "If you are willing and obedient, you shall eat the good of the land" (Is 1:19 NKJV). In other words, I realize all God has for me, spiritually, socially and economically. Youth, you do not have to compromise, short-change, circumvent or even feel different; You are different; remember, you are a royal priesthood, a chosen generation, a peculiar people. As such, you cannot continue to be sensual, operate on and by your five senses; rather you must operate by and with the supernatural, the Spirit of the Living God.

However, your difference is not in what you wear or the bling-bling; rather, your difference and the difference in you is the result of your salvation and godly Christian character.

This is nothing to be ashamed of; rather, it is something to be proud of. As a believer, you are automatically different, your Christian belief distinguishes you from non-believers; you do not talk, walk or act as others who do not believe. You operate in a spirit of supernatural excellence and godly authority.

Now, being different does not make you any better. Why not? Because who you are in Christ is what makes you different. Also, because believers already know this has absolutely nothing to do with their ability to do well or be good; it has all to do with <u>salvation</u> and <u>obedience</u> to the call and will of God. And as you obey Almighty God, you are entitled with and to his activation (the Holy Spirit) and the receiving of the full benefits and promises as his son, king, and priest. Remember, God loads us with benefits daily. Blessed be the Lord who loads us with benefits, the God of our salvation (Ps 68:19). You cannot be denied for you are an <u>heir</u> and <u>joint heir</u> with Christ Jesus; thus you, child of God, have an inheritance and have been blessed with all spiritual blessings in heavenly places (Eph 1:3) (the spiritual realm). Truly, young people, to enjoy the real benefits of God and impact your generation you must obey His call (purpose) to fulfill your purpose and destiny by being willing and obedient to His divine calling on your life. Young people, exercise your God-given talents, experiences and overwhelming presence of God's supernatural provision (resources) to fulfill your purpose, legacy and destiny. Amazingly, many of us, including you, are missing so much in our lives because of one simple principle. That principle is "obey"; obedience to the commandments, principles and precepts of God and His instruction manual. The Bible records in Isaiah1:19, "If we are willing and obedient; we will enjoy the fat of the land." Remember, young people, because the earth is the Lord's, it is ours also, for God has given us, his children, sons, daughters, priests, kings and believers authority over the earth. We just need to exercise that authority in what we say and do. Young people, what's happening? Please understand that God loads us with benefits daily. Are we going to sit around and hoard them, or are we going to share the wealth and benefits with those who are less fortunate than ourselves? God's plan of universal <u>sowing</u> and <u>reaping</u> is what we all need to operate in and through His Kingdom. Youth, readers, you will only receive to the level you are willing to give. In other words, if you sow (give) meagerly, then you will receive correspondingly the same. Conversely, if you give abundantly, you will receive the same.

I believe the best policy and practice would be to share; for God loved us so much that he shared his only begotten (first born) son that we might have life and life more abundantly. Thus we, you, are beneficiaries from his love for us. Young people, let's love and share in our actions through what we do and say. Remember, if you are willing (available) and obedient (obey), you will enjoy the fullness of God's sovereign kingdom. Please be advised that our fatness (fullness) manifestation of God's grace is not necessarily for us; but it is for us to bless others. I believe that you will agree with me that we all come short and are deficient in this area. What most of us do is seek to get, but we are reluctant to release and sow, thus our continued ability to receive is limited by our own selfish self-centeredness. Please understand and be ever mindful that if you want to be great and enjoy all that God has for you, you must be willing and obedient; only then will you enjoy the fat of the land (universe). I believe you have gotten the drift. Remember, "give and it will be given to you: good measure, pressed down, shaken together, and running over will be put into your bosom – your wealthy place" (Lk 6:38 NKJV).

BENEFITS

Interestingly, it seems that we all are trying to get the good benefits that God has for all of us; yet it seems that our "hunger" and thirst is diminishing for God. And we are not agonizing and anguishing for our fellow brothers and sisters who are lost and have no knowledge or desire for Christ. As I talk, travel, and interact with people on the church, <u>local</u>, <u>state</u>, <u>national</u>, and <u>international scene</u>, I realize that there is one common thread that weaves all of us together; people are looking for the authenticity (realness) and evidence (results) of this almighty God we say we serve. People are looking for the God in us. We say we serve an Almighty God, but there is no evidence in many of our lives. The world, the lost, are looking for and expecting to see a witness for the signs, wonders and miracles that we believers talk about. Many of lives are in shambles, jacked-up, broken, busted and disgusted. Young people, and anyone reading this page, please realize that we, the believers, are the <u>visible manifestation</u> of the <u>invisible God</u> in the earthly realm; as such, we, the believers, in many cases will be the only image of God the lost will see and recognize; and yes, the lost has the capacity to recognize the real from the not real. That's why it is so important to always be real and operate with Kingdom power. Thus, we must always be <u>vigilant,</u> at attention on our <u>spiritual duty</u> and <u>attentive</u> to serve and share the Good News of the Gospel of Jesus Christ. As it made a difference in our lives when they see us, it will automatically make a difference in their lives in their lost state.

People from all walks of life are <u>hungering</u> and <u>searching</u> for true evidence of godly Kingdom benefits. Let us be who God has created us to be by telling the world of God benefits, and then being <u>a living demonstration</u> of God's manifested, demonstrated presence. For God truly loads us with benefits daily. Now, youth, "roll" with me for a moment: What do you think is a major reason there is <u>youth violence,</u> <u>lewd and looseness</u> of <u>behavior</u> and lack of <u>fundamental and foundational individual</u> and <u>collective discipline</u> in our world today? While there are many reasons, one of the primary reasons is the lack of <u>parental guidance, training, home training, reinforcement</u> and a mindset and mentality of what am I going to get; what's in it for me? There is lack of respect for authority and lack of identify (knowing who you/they are).

Young people, do not fall for or succumb to this ill-thought mind-set of reaping where you have not sown. In other words, in order to receive and obtain lasting benefits and blessings, you must be willing and obedient to the call of Almighty God. Anything less than that will be temporal, and you will never experience the eternal lasting blessings and empowerment of Almighty God. So, let's now conduct some self-evaluation/assessment as to what you are looking for more. Surely, if you are rightly related to Christ, then you have eternal status with your heavenly Father, Jesus the Christ. Now, for many of you, you are probably saying to yourself and others, I cannot relate or feel right about my Heavenly Father, because my earthly father was never there for me and my siblings. Youth, I cannot say that <u>I understand,</u> <u>feel,</u> or <u>can relate to your situation</u>. I say this because my father was always home and in my life. What I can say to you is that for those of you who believe Almighty God, your Heavenly Father will never leave or forsake you. Now remember that he is a loving, kind, compassionate and caring Father. So, all of you who desire a true, lasting friend that will always be there, God Almighty, Abba Father, is always there. For He said that He would never leave or forsake us, that even if we make our bed in Hell, He will be there with us also. He is faithful, and we can trust Him to the end of the age. Youth, that is a Father! Certainly, I am not naïve enough to think or say to you that yes, because God created us relational to each other, we periodically do need a hug/embrace and some <u>affirmation</u> and <u>confirmation</u> here on earth. As such, what you need to ask is for God to send Christian/God-fearing, dedicated men and women into your lives. Understand that because God is faithful, he will make this happen because "He is faithful to his word (Ps 119:89 NKJV), and always remember that God's word is forever settled in Heaven. Youth, what you must understand and accept is that because God has blessed us with all spiritual blessing in heavenly places, and because he loads us with benefits daily, this should not be a concern of ours at all, "for God is not a man that he should lie; or the Son of Man that he should repent"(Nm 23:19 NKJV), for what God promised, He is also able to deliver, for He is not slack on His promises; and those of us that come to Him, must believe that "He is a rewarder of those of us that diligently seek Him" (Heb 11:6 NKJV). Understanding <u>who we are</u>, <u>what we are</u> and what our ultimate destination is should give all of us (believers) an undeniable assurance that being concerned about benefits is truly not an issue for the child of God; the King of Kings. Seemingly, because you, youth, do not understand that we are citizens of heaven and not permanent citizens of Planet Earth, conversely, it is mind boggling as to what you could and should do, youth, if this vital point was taken under divine guidance. For you see, because God has made <u>irrevocable promises</u> to and for us; thus, our insatiable quest for temporal earthly benefits would cease, and all of us would understand that Almighty God has us fully covered and protected for us and with "exceedingly abundantly blessings above and beyond anything that we could ask or think according to the power that works in us" (Eph 3:20 NJKV). Young people, because the Almighty God lives in us through the presence and person of the Holy Spirit, we have all the benefits we need. So, young people, let's get moving and make an impact on your generation now. Because our God is Faithful, you should and must be willing and obedient. From this life-long posture, you are promised by God Almighty that you will enjoy the (Fat-Fullness) of everything on Planet Earth. The real issue is to take care of what God would have you take care of; and concurrently, you are and will be taken care of likewise by God. Accordingly, youth, let's get with it and make a difference. Biblically speaking, the Scripture record that the strong must bear the infirmities of the weak. Yes, you and I are our brother's keepers. Whereas I realize this is a heavy burden to carry sometimes, nevertheless, it can and must be done. Follow me for a moment; the strong (persuaded, -convinced) are those who have and are following Christ and making a difference now in their generation. The weak (unsure/wavering) are not convinced that God is able to deliver them from any fiery furnace, situation or circumstance. Moreover, the strong are those who will go forth; show to or not knowing where they might be ordered, but yet God will only lead them through the path of and to righteousness and a smooth path to unprecedented victory. Further, young people, when you really understand how great and awesome Christ is, then the benefits will not really matter because you, like me, know that your "stuff" is already taken care of. Now, because you are assured that God is not slack on His Promises, "but without faith it is impossible to please Him, for he who comes to God must believe that He is, and that He is a rewarder of those who diligently seek Him" (Heb 11:6 NKJV),; you can now be about the Kingdom Business of leaving a lasting legacy for the next generation. So, because I fully and completely understand that God has my total life under control and taken care of, I can now focus on truly being a godly success, but more importantly, significantly (enduringly) impacting my generation and for upcoming, forthcoming generations. Remember, youth, the Scripture records that a "Good Man" leaves an inheritance for his children and children's children (Prv 13:22). Youth, will you leave an inheritance for the next generation? Please understand that we must think about and become producers of goods and services and dispel and destroy the mindset of being consumers and not producers. In other words, renounce the idea that I must buy everything that I see and keep up with all the latest and greatest gadgets and fashions. I know that you will answer the call as myself; you shall leave a lasting legacy, because you will leave a legacy—will it be <u>successful</u> or <u>significant</u>? You see, success in most cases is temporary, whereas significance is lasting. Be significant.

CHAPTER FIVE
LEGACY (SOLIDIFIED REMEMBRANCE)

As youth and young people, part of an ever-emerging and changing generation, you will leave a destiny (conclusion), generational and trans-generational wealth for your family. What am I saying, well, it is really simple; if you look back in and on your history and child rearing, most of us,; particularly Americans of African descent, started out with nothing from our biological fathers and mothers and left most of us with no tangible wealth or seed. Thus, most of us have continued that process; we must say and demand that cycle stops with us and our generation.

More specifically, as a baby-boomer myself, when I graduated from high school I was not given or inherited anything other than go to school, graduate, and make a lot of money. Well, again, that did not happen either, and will not happen necessarily in that sequence, yet it will happen and is happening supernaturally. However, through strategic thinking and entrepreneurial business vehicles and tools I am working toward leaving a legacy of generational and trans-generational wealth for my family. The other scenario is working for someone else. Understand that having a job is honorable. This may and probably is a starting point for many of us. What I say to you is, having an entrance and exit plan from a job to a business is what you really need. Often, you may work a job too long and not become an entrepreneur; we must be business-minded entrepreneurs and start businesses, both individual and family owned. Now, do not misunderstand me. I am forever grateful and thankful for what my parents did, for they instilled something in me that was much more precious; my parents instilled in me that I could accomplish any task or feat if I put my mind to it (focus). They further instilled <u>wisdom</u>, <u>self-worth</u>, and <u>determination</u>; and that if I obtained an education, it could not be taken away from me by anybody. Well, such is the case. I obtained an education, and yes, it cannot be taken away from me; and yes, it has and continues to help me immeasurably in my daily walk and life. Moreover, I am an entrepreneur, and I will fulfill the biblical mandate on my life and leave an inheritance for my children and children's children.

Young people, if you are to leave a lasting legacy long after you die, you must set and maintain some very high standards; compromise is not an option. Understand that spiritually and biblically, the Scripture/Holy Spirit states that "a good man leaves an inheritance for his children and children's children." That is for generations that godly men must touch; if you do not touch four generations, you will be considered a failure. In order for this to happen, youth, please understand there are certain things you must do now. A good, solid, biblical, spiritual and high self-value-based foundation must be laid to support your future growth. What you must do includes but is not limited to the following: You must understand that life is not <u>microwavable</u>, and you must dispel the idea that immediate gratification (IG Complex) will not come quickly. While God has already completed everything, many of us must go through a process, so the IG Complex may not necessarily come quickly; God is a God of process. Significance comes through progressive forward movement, trials, tribulations and undaunted focus on God and godly principles, entrepreneurial principles and guidelines.

Legacy (Solidified Remembrance)

Youth, life is a forward-moving process, and journey; it is full of <u>appointments,</u> <u>disappointment,</u> <u>dissatisfactions,</u> and a multitude of other surprising distractions if you do not stay focused. Because of the distractions that life throws at us, it is so vitally important that you and I stay focused on our purpose (calling), destiny and legacy. It is not easy, but we must stay on point and remain in our divine, godly position we have been placed in. Position is so important; when you are in your godly position ,the power and authority of Almighty God is with and on you to do supernatural exploits. In some cases, we must learn to play the hand we are dealt; while the hand we were dealt may not be good yet, we can make a bad hand *good;* it all depends on how we play it. It is amazing how the natural world that we all live in makes and leaves in most cases a devastating impact on the world in such a negative way, and many of us are spiritually and physically blind to what is actually happening. For instance, there have been rap artists murdered, and their destructive music and lyrics continue to captivate youth today. We must get and regain the total attention of our youth today by being authentic, living demonstrations of the only True and Living God; and that God is greater and wiser than the rap artists and their temporary attractions and music.

Yet many well-deserving youth with the best of intentions are never given or even have a desire to impact their generation with godly attributes or character to follow because of the obsession with the lyrics of "popular music."

<u>Youth of destiny</u>, you must impact your generation and society in a lasting, impactful way. The objective of the unsaved and un-churched is to destroy the godly seed that is up and coming. To bring the point more specifically home, look at the daily murders that are being committed by youth of all ages, particularly African Americans. To give you a few examples, the Virginia Tech massacre where thirty-two innocent youth were murdered; the Newark, New Jersey, incident where a fifteen-year-old youth shot three innocent young teenagers in the head, execution style. What is wrong? Well, it appears that there is no understanding, care or regard for authority or human life; and more importantly, a lack of understanding of our legacy. Youth, you must wake up to the reality of the consequences of your actions and understand that <u>un-thought-out, knee-jerk reactions</u> can and will lead to a lifetime of negative consequences and results.

Many of you are spiritually, socially, and economically aware of this out-of-control pandemic and cycle of <u>killings</u>, <u>booty</u>

shaking, tattooing, and consumer-minded, extreme-thinking-minded generation can be changed. It can be changed by you making a new move now. It is up to you; use your God-given talents, influence and determination to turn around this runaway force of out of control youth. Youth, I know and believe that you can stop what this new negative mindset is about. Its sole purpose is to take your generation out. Youth, impact (make and be different) your environment, work assignment, high school, college or wherever you find yourself. For the change must occur now; you are a new generation to create a revolution for a reformation. Now, reign, rule, and take dominion and authority, for those of us who know our God shall be strong and do great exploits (take over) do not take sides, but take over, now takeover! "But the people who know their God shall be strong, and carry out great exploits" (Dn 11:32 NKJV).

UNDERSTAND YOUR MISSION

What am I to do? Good question; I'm glad you asked. Well, you are not to do what you have been doing because it is not working. Youth, as astute and wise as you are, insanity is doing the same thing over and over again and expecting different results. Youth, your mission is to impact, transition, make a lasting impact, difference and significance in your generation, society, and peers. Understanding your mission must drive you to be different, not necessarily in appearance but spiritually, in what you say and do. You do not need to create anything new; everything you need is supernaturally implanted deep within you, for the Holy Spirit has made a life-long <u>deposit</u> and <u>impartation</u> that continues to get stronger in you. Yes, youth, you will make an impact and change your generation, now!

Changing a generation is not going to be easy, yet it is possible. Remember, every opportunity that I have, I must take full advantage of in order to make a difference. Also, I must be consistent and persistent and follow through on all my assignments and opportunities to witness and make Kingdom disciples. This is so important that missing opportunities may not allow me to come in contact with or even be exposed to the same opportunity again.

SUCCESS OR SIGNIFANCE

Seemingly, in most instances the <u>advent</u> and <u>quest</u> to succeed in our temporal world have caused many of us—and yes, youth—to compromise your values and integrity. Youth, there appears to be some <u>confusion</u> and <u>misunderstanding</u> as to what is more important, <u>success</u> or <u>significance</u>. Well, I know you are asking the question, what is the difference between the two? Let's explore the meaning of both. <u>Success</u> by this worldly present day standards is measured primarily by how much stuff—material possessions, bling, property and tangibles—one can amass. Now, while truly there is nothing wrong with having stuff, the issue is that the stuff should not have, possess or control us. The sobering reality is that in most cases, the stuff rules us, rather than us ruling the stuff. Now, let's explore significance. Significance is primarily what you cannot see; it is an intangible that manifests tangibles in an unlimited fashion. Youth, I venture to state that when you evaluate both success and significance, you will choose to be significant. Please understand, in no way am I saying do not set some <u>goals</u>, <u>objectives</u> and <u>strategies</u>. For in order for anything to be accomplished there must be <u>plans</u>, <u>goals</u>, <u>objectives</u>, and <u>milestones</u> for assessment and evaluation. So, youth, set those goals and objectives and plans; write them down. Write the vision and make it plain on tablets, that he may run who reads it. "For the vision is yet for an appointed time; but at the end it will speak, and it will not lie. Though it tarries, wait for it; because it will surely come, it will not tarry" (Hb 2:2-3 NKJV).

The most important part of it all is to stay focused on the bottom line; that is what will impact your generation, for before I/you were formed in our mother's womb,; we were ordained prophets to nations; and through that godly ordination we are <u>empowered</u> to <u>impact</u> everything within our sphere of influence. Because you are now intimately familiar with and understand the vital importance of <u>improving</u>, <u>clarifying</u>, and <u>fulfilling</u> your <u>legacy</u>, <u>mission</u>, <u>purpose</u> and <u>destiny</u> <u>individually</u>, <u>collectively</u> and <u>corporately</u>, you can appreciate the importance and necessity of being and making a lasting impression on all with whom you come in contact. So, are you going to be overshadowed by temporal success or eternal significance? Young people/reader, you are living in the most interesting, best of and exciting times, for now/today is your/our finest hour. While circumstances appear to be dark, bleak, cloudy and gloomy, our God still reigns and rules. Please do not be hoodwinked and/or bamboozled or have the wool pulled over your eyes thinking that if you are not part of or participate in this all-<u>consuming</u>, <u>consumer-minded</u> <u>spending, get-all-I-can, Now generation, you become nobody</u>. Youth, *this is a trick* from the wiles, cunningness, craftiness of the devil himself, straight from the pit of Hell. Admit it, we all have <u>goals, aspirations</u>, things we would like to accomplish in this life, and that is a good thing. However, the key is to understand that while you can and should be a success, the more and important issue is to make it crystal clear to yourself and others that you must without fail be significant—that is, leave a lasting and permanent imprint (significance) after your physical death. And yes, youth, we all will die; it is a matter of when. The issue is to be prepared to transition. The key is asking are you/we ready, and have we made the lasting difference of being significant? Now, I am sure you are asking, how do I become significant in this wild and out of control world? <u>Great question</u>; I am glad that you asked. Well, please understand, being significant is really not something you do; it is really who you are and have been created to be. Remember, as Spirit-filled believers of the Lord Jesus Christ, you have the DNA of Almighty God, Jesus the Christ; how can you be anything other than significant? <u>Discovering, uncovering</u> your destiny is probably the most difficult thing you will experience and encounter. The process is that once you discover what your destiny and purpose are, it becomes a matter of walking (journeying) out this destiny in everything that you do, at school, work, home, vacation, and marketplace and during your leisure time. Surprisingly, you will be amazed and mind boggled as to who is watching you, and how many people you are impacting either negatively or positively. Many millions, hundreds, thousands will be touched during your journey and lifetime. As such, your journey pilgrimage and Christian walk will suddenly realize and evidence that you are being, living and becoming significant in your own time; a true Legacy. Youth, being and becoming significant is what you must be determined to be; it must be intentional. You do not think about it; you do it. In other words, you must make your effort; an intentional action, for it will not automatically happen. You must be determined and persevere now. Understand that everything around and outside of us is really designed to shut us completely down, render us immobilized and further make us insignificant. I remind each of you that in order to be significant you must stay focused and intentionally press/stretch forward, exceeding and surpassing all odds.

Young people, while we/you are living in what may seem like the worst of times, we really are living in the best of times. I am sure you are asking, how could you possibly say that? Well, we are living in the best of times because the *Kingdom of God is not subject to the seemingly bad economic times.* Recession and famine may appear to be and to some degree may be in the world; however, we, the sons and daughters of the Most High God, can be assured that we shall be taken care of, even in famine, "God says we will be satisfied in the midst of a famine" (Ps 37:19). Remember, "Beloved, I pray that you may prosper in all things and be in health, just as your soul prospers (3 Jn 1:2 NKJV). It is God's will that His people prosper and be in good health, even as our souls prosper. So if we are believing and trusting God, then this is the time to take full advantage of and gain what appears to be a famine in the land. Youth, it is truly <u>refreshing</u>, <u>humbling</u> and <u>encouraging</u> to know that whatever is going on, we the believers can be and should be assured that God has promised us that He will never leave or forsake us. Now, that promise cannot be obtained or received from anyone else; it is irrevocable. It could not be changed even if God wanted to. The Now issue is to remain <u>focused</u>, <u>dedicated</u> and <u>committed</u> and <u>preserve</u> to the end of our journey. "Remember, The race is not to the swift, nor the battle to the strong, nor bread to the wise, nor riches to men of understanding, nor favor to men of skill; but time and chance happen to them all" (Eccl 9:11b NKJV). So

I challenge each of you to endure to the end and be significant in and for your generation and beyond, making a lasting impact and creating an imprint that cannot be erased. Young people, take full and unparalleled advantage of every opportunity and be significant; leave a lasting legacy today. Now be it, and see it happening right before your very eyes. Remember you and I are truly empowered to impact our culture, environment, and the world.

www.ingramcontent.com/pod-product-compliance
Ingram Content Group UK Ltd.
Pitfield, Milton Keynes, MK11 3LW, UK
UKHW022221230426
12048UKWH00016BA/984